# EXPLORERS IN
# AFRICA

USBORNE PUBLISHING

## Acknowledgements

We wish to thank the following individuals and organizations for their assistance and for making available material in their collections.

Key to picture positions: (T) top (C) centre (L) left (R) right

Dr. John Baker p. 24—5
Bibliothèque Nationale p. 4—5(TC) (BL)
British Museum p. 10(TL)(TC)(TR), 15(TR), 21(B), 39(BR), 41(T), 42(CR)(BR), 43(T), 46
Oliver Carruthers p. 18(TR)(CL), 40(B), 41(B)
Jean-Loup Charmet, Paris p. 33(B, second from right)
Church Missionary Society p. 20(TR)(TL)
David & Charles Ltd, from Yesterday's Shopping p. 26(BL)
Mary Evans Picture Library p. 33(B, second from left), 34(TC), 44(TL)
Robert Harding Associates p. 21(T), 30(CR)
Keystone p. 45(TR)(CR)(BR)
Mansell Collection p. 30(TL)
Museu Nacional de Arte Antigua, Lisbon p. 4(TL)
National Maritime Museum, Greenwich p. 12(BR)
National Portrait Gallery p. 8(BL), 18(TL), 22(TL)
Popperfoto p. 4(TC)
Radio Times Hulton Picture Library p. 31(RC), 37(CL)
Royal Commonwealth Society p. 6(TR), 8(TR), 30(B), 33(BR)(BL), 40(TL), 44(BL)
Royal Geographical Society p. 9(BR), 22(C), 28(TL)
Richard Stanley Collection p. 36(L)
Rijksmuseum voor Volkenjunde, Leiden p. 39(BL)(BC)(BR)
South African Embassy, London p. 14(TL)(TC), 44(CL) both pictures
Spink & Son Ltd. p. 16(TL), 17(CR)
The White Fathers p. 20(TC)

## Illustrators and Photographers

Peter Bailey
Stephen Bennett
Bernard Blatch
David Bushaway
Cheryl Drower
Peter Henville
David Jefferis
Pat Ludlow
Brian Marshall
John Martin Studio
Denis Moore
John P. Mousdale
Mark Peppé
Mike Roffe
John Smith
Ron Stenberg
John Thompson
Jenny Thorne
Ultima

**Editor** Sue Jacquemier
**Picture Manager** Millicent Trowbridge
**Picture Research** Anne Hithersay
**Art Director** John Strange

First published in 1975
by Usborne Publishing Ltd
20 Garrick Street, London WC2

© text: Richard Hall
© artwork: Usborne Publishing Ltd
Made and printed in England by Hazell Watson & Viney Ltd, Aylesbury, Bucks
ISBN 0 86020 013 2

# EXPLORERS IN
# AFRICA
## RICHARD HALL

# CONTENTS

| | |
|---|---|
| 4 | The African Outline |
| 6 | Dangers of the Interior |
| 8 | Into the Dark Continent |
| 10 | Discovering Africa's People |
| 12 | The Slave Trade |
| 14 | South Africa's White Settlers |
| 16 | Trade and the Travellers |
| 18 | Livingstone—the Early Years |
| 20 | Muslims and Christians |
| 22 | The Nile Mystery |
| 24 | Samuel and Florence Baker |
| 26 | An Explorer's Kit |
| 28 | The Death of Livingstone |
| 30 | Scientific Explorers |
| 32 | Stanley—from Zanzibar to Banana Point |
| 34 | Women Travellers |
| 36 | The Rescue of Emin Pasha |
| 38 | The Africans' View of the Explorers |
| 40 | Naturalist's Notebook |
| 42 | Archaeologist Explorers |
| 44 | Africa—1914 to 1970 |
| 46 | Time Chart—Africa's Explorers |
| 47 | Index |

# The African Outline

▲ **Henry the Navigator.**
In 1416 he began the Portuguese sea voyages to find gold in Africa and a route to India.

▲ **Vasco da Gama**
completed the work of sailing around Africa from west to east in 1497–9.

◄ **Compasses** were used for navigation after about 1500. Earlier Portuguese sailors found the true north with a lodestone. (magnetic oxide of iron).

## The Portuguese explorers

The Europeans knew almost nothing about Africa, a huge continent on their doorstep, until 500 years ago. In ancient times the Phoenicians—Middle Eastern traders and seafarers—had made journeys down the west and east African coasts, and one expedition went right around the continent. But that was forgotten. By A.D. 800, the Arabs controlled all the northern coastline from Egypt to the straits of Gibraltar, and Arab towns dotted the east coast. Since the Europeans were always fighting the Muslim Arabs, Africa was "enemy-occupied territory" to Christians.

But by 1400, Europe was on the attack. The Arabs were driven from Spain; in 1415 the North African port of Ceuta was captured by Prince Henry of Portugal. He decided to find a way round Africa to India, famous for its spices and jewels. The route overland through Asia was controlled by Muslims and Mongols. Henry did not guess that the Portuguese ships would have to go as far south of the Equator as he was to the north of it in order to reach India by sea. Ship after ship ventured along the barren Morrocan coast; many were wrecked. Henry died in 1460, but the work of exploration he had started was kept going. In 1482, Captain Diego Cam reached the mouth of the Congo River and two years later went 1,500 miles further south, but died on the voyage.

The Cape of Good Hope was reached at last by Bartholomew Diaz in 1487, and ten years afterwards Vasco da Gama sailed around Africa and across the Indian Ocean. In the same decade, Christopher Columbus had sailed across the Atlantic, also looking for a sea route to the Indies. To halt the rivalry between Spain and Portugal, the Pope decreed that the Spaniards should rule the Americas, the Portuguese Africa and the Orient.

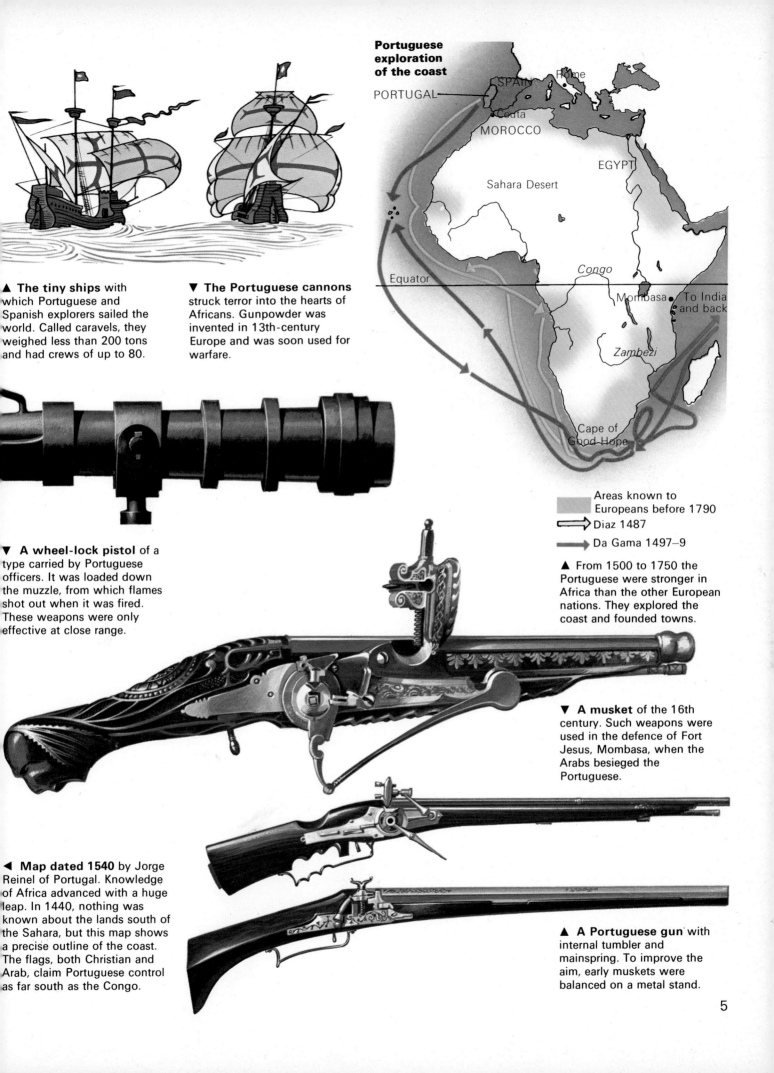

**Portuguese exploration of the coast**

SPAIN
PORTUGAL
Rome
Ceuta
MOROCCO
EGYPT
Sahara Desert
Equator
Congo
Mombasa
To India and back
Zambezi
Cape of Good Hope

Areas known to Europeans before 1790
Diaz 1487
Da Gama 1497–9

▲ **The tiny ships** with which Portuguese and Spanish explorers sailed the world. Called caravels, they weighed less than 200 tons and had crews of up to 80.

▼ **The Portuguese cannons** struck terror into the hearts of Africans. Gunpowder was invented in 13th-century Europe and was soon used for warfare.

▼ **A wheel-lock pistol** of a type carried by Portuguese officers. It was loaded down the muzzle, from which flames shot out when it was fired. These weapons were only effective at close range.

◀ **Map dated 1540** by Jorge Reinel of Portugal. Knowledge of Africa advanced with a huge leap. In 1440, nothing was known about the lands south of the Sahara, but this map shows a precise outline of the coast. The flags, both Christian and Arab, claim Portuguese control as far south as the Congo.

▲ From 1500 to 1750 the Portuguese were stronger in Africa than the other European nations. They explored the coast and founded towns.

▼ **A musket** of the 16th century. Such weapons were used in the defence of Fort Jesus, Mombasa, when the Arabs besieged the Portuguese.

▲ **A Portuguese gun** with internal tumbler and mainspring. To improve the aim, early muskets were balanced on a metal stand.

5

# Dangers of the Interior

Africa was the last continent to give up its secrets. Many lives were lost in trying to explore the interior. As recently as 100 years ago vast regions on maps of Africa were left completely blank. The geographers could only write on areas far bigger than all of Europe "Terra Incognita"—Unknown Lands.

Apart from some adventurous Arab scholars and merchants, the main outsiders who went exploring in Africa were the Europeans. They left Africa until last for several reasons. One was that until the 19th century the stronger European powers, such as Britain, France and Spain, were kept busy colonizing the Americas and India. The rewards to be won in Africa were less plain.

For many centuries, the Europeans stayed away from Africa because of the physical dangers. Whichever way you tried to tackle it, Africa was hard to get into. The seemingly easiest way would have been to sail up its rivers to the high plateau covering most of the interior. However, the Congo, Zambezi and Nile could not be navigated because of rapids and cateracts. The Niger's mouth could not be found in the dense mangrove swamps around its estuary. Along much of the coastline were tropical jungles— humid, trackless and causing fevers that were often fatal to white travellers.

In the north was the great barrier of the Sahara Desert, 3,500 miles wide from the Atlantic to the Nile. The shortest route across it from Tripoli to Lake Chad was more than 1,000 miles. For many centuries there had been caravan routes from oasis to oasis, using camels (first imported from Asia by the Romans). But Europeans trying to explore across the Sahara met hostility from the Muslims, unwilling to give "infidels" the secrets of the desert trade. As for wildlife, some animals were a source of food, but others were an added hazard for white travellers.

◄ **René Caillié** was one of several European travellers who disguised himself as an Arab to explore North Africa. He reached Timbuktu in 1827 by pretending to be an Egyptian. Caillié crossed the Sahara with a camel caravan. He became a French national hero.

▲ **The most feared nomads** of the desert were the Tuaregs, who readily killed foreigners for their possessions. The picture above is from an 1821 travellers' guide by Captain G. F. Lyon. Further south in Africa, tribal chiefs demanded tribute in cloth and guns from explorers.

▲ **The mosquito** was Africa's secret weapon against outsiders. Until 1894, nobody knew what caused malaria, which was blamed—as its name suggests—on "bad air". Some protection was given by quinine, first used in 1854 by William Baikie in Nigeria.

▶ **Modes of tropical travel:** donkeys survived best, and camels were less successful. Canoes could be carried between rivers. Hammocks were used by the sick and by women. Walking in the sun was more comfortable with a parasol.

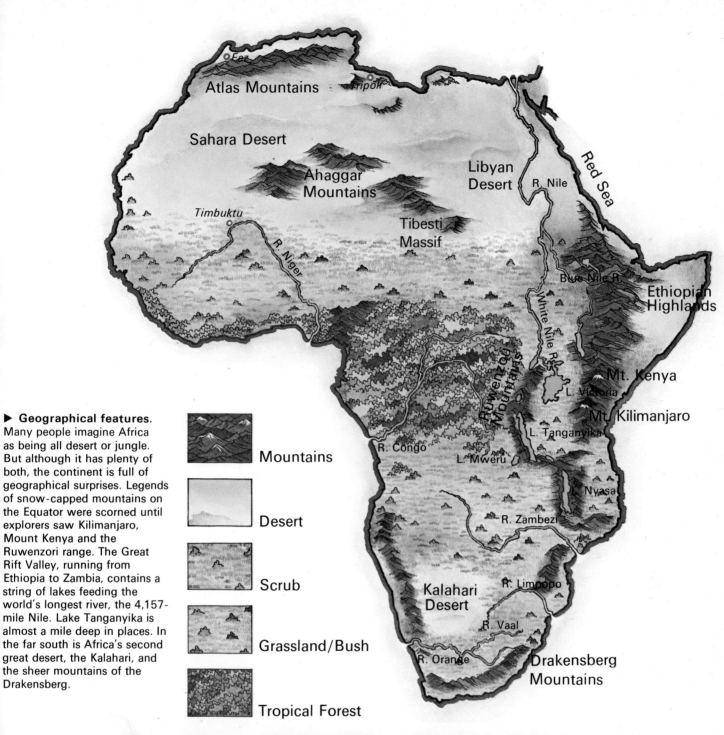

Atlas Mountains

Fez

Tripoli

Sahara Desert

Ahaggar
Mountains

Libyan
Desert

R. Nile

Red Sea

Timbuktu

R. Niger

Tibesti
Massif

Blue Nile R.

Ethiopian
Highlands

White Nile R.

Ruwenzori
Mountains

Mt. Kenya

L. Victoria

Mt. Kilimanjaro

L. Tanganyika

R. Congo

L. Mweru

Nyasa

R. Zambezi

R. Limpopo

Kalahari
Desert

R. Vaal

R. Orange

Drakensberg
Mountains

▶ **Geographical features.**
Many people imagine Africa
as being all desert or jungle.
But although it has plenty of
both, the continent is full of
geographical surprises. Legends
of snow-capped mountains on
the Equator were scorned until
explorers saw Kilimanjaro,
Mount Kenya and the
Ruwenzori range. The Great
Rift Valley, running from
Ethiopia to Zambia, contains a
string of lakes feeding the
world's longest river, the 4,157-
mile Nile. Lake Tanganyika is
almost a mile deep in places. In
the far south is Africa's second
great desert, the Kalahari, and
the sheer mountains of the
Drakensberg.

Mountains

Desert

Scrub

Grassland/Bush

Tropical Forest

# Into the Dark Continent

▲ **James Bruce,** a tall, broad Scot, nicknamed "Man Mountain", explored Ethiopia in the 18th century.

▶ **A canja,** the two-masted boat in which Bruce sailed down the Nile. He then crossed to the Red Sea, and entered Ethiopia. Travelling by horse he reached Lake Tana and the source of the Blue Nile.

◀ **Mungo Park** qualified as a doctor and travelled in the Far East before going to West Africa at the age of 23. After learning Arabic he set off from a British trading post 200 miles inland towards Ségou on the Niger River.

▼ **Routes** of the early explorers and the first crossing of the continent by two Portuguese half-castes.

Cairo
EGYPT
Red Sea
R. Nile
R. Niger
Massawa
Ségou
L. Tana
WEST AFRICA
ETHIOPIA
SOMALIA
R. Congo
Equator
ANGOLA
Teto
MOZAMBIQUE
R. Zambezi

De Lacerda 1798 ⟹
Park 1795–7 ⟹
Bruce 1769–72 ⟹
Baptista and José 1802–10 ⟹

▶ **Park** suffered terrifying encounters, including this meeting with a lion, on his 1,500-mile journey in 1795-7. At one point he was robbed of everything: "I saw myself in the midst of a vast wilderness in the depth of the rainy season, naked and alone . . . I was 500 miles from the nearest European settlements." But Park struggled back to the coast and brought to Europe the first eye-witness account of the Great Niger.

## Bruce and Park

The first Europeans who tried to find out what lay inland in Africa were Portuguese missionaries. Between 1500 and 1600 they made journeys into Angola and Mozambique, but their discoveries were forgotten. In Ethiopia, the Portuguese were more successful, for a time, and the Ethiopian emperor was converted to Catholicism. Even that did not last—in 1633 the Portuguese were expelled from Ethiopia for ever.

It was now the turn of the British, who were gaining strength as a world power. A Scotsman, James Bruce, read several Portuguese books on Ethiopia and decided to go there and find the source of the Blue Nile. Bruce was a completely new kind of African traveller—he was not interested in trade, missionary work or colonies. *He went to find out.* Also, he kept accurate records about everything he saw. Bruce's journey (1769–72) took him through the Red Sea, across Ethiopia and down the Nile to Cairo. But when he returned to London his descriptions of these explorations were doubted, especially his account of an Ethiopian banquet where guests ate raw steaks cut from a live ox. He was a very bad-tempered man who made many enemies, so his achievements were disputed until his book was published in five volumes in 1790 just before his death.

Even so, Bruce's journey led to the founding of the Association for Promoting the Discovery of the Interior Parts of Africa, in 1788. In 1795, the Association found another Scot, Mungo Park, eager to go exploring. He was sent to look for the course of the Niger River. Park's first journey up the Gambia River and across country to the Niger took two years. He was imprisoned, and almost died of fever and hunger. But he returned to Britain and wrote a brilliant account of his travels. Six years later he went back to West Africa, but he was drowned after sailing 1,000 miles down the Niger.

▲ **The folding blunderbuss** Bruce took with him. He hid it beneath his robes when he was wearing Arab dress.

▶ **Bruce's telescope.** A keen astronomer, Bruce caused amazement in Ethiopia by forecasting an eclipse of the moon. In the desert, most of his possessions had to be abandoned, but he clung on to this telescope.

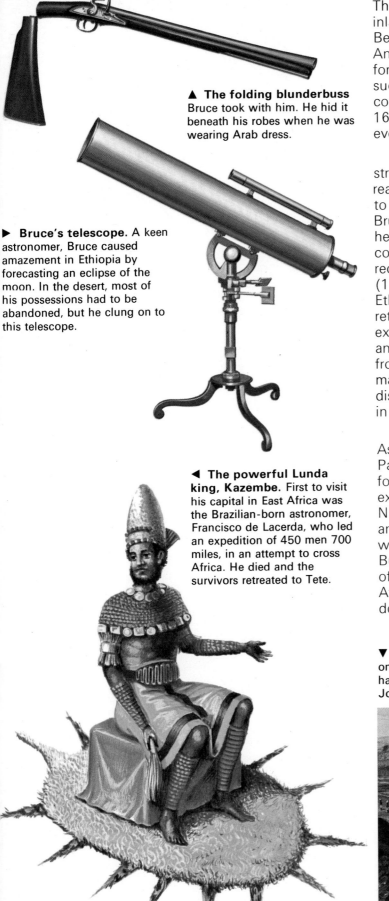

◀ **The powerful Lunda king, Kazembe.** First to visit his capital in East Africa was the Brazilian-born astronomer, Francisco de Lacerda, who led an expedition of 450 men 700 miles, in an attempt to cross Africa. He died and the survivors retreated to Tete.

▼ **Tete,** a Portuguese outpost on the Zambezi. In 1810, two half-castes named Baptista and José reached Tete from Angola. On the way they were imprisoned by Kazembe for four years. They also made a return journey across Africa.

# Discovering Africa's People

Exploring a continent means discovering the people as well as looking for rivers and mountains; but some explorers understood little about African customs or the Africans' way of life.

▲ **Carved soapstone head** from Sherbro Island in Sierra Leone. Small stone figures were buried in the rice-fields to bring a good crop.

▲ **A wooden stool**, carved for a chief of the Kuba people in the Congo. African craftsmen followed designs handed down from father to son.

▼ **Bush spirit mask** from West Africa. Carvings dating back more than 2,000 years have been found in Nigeria.

▲ **Ivory leopard** from Benin. Benin art was first known to Europe 80 years ago, after British troops seized many sculptures.

▶ **The small hand piano** is one of Africa's most popular musical instruments. There are also many kinds of drums, flutes and harps.

▶ Not all Africans are black; nor are their features all alike. Some Africans, such as the Negroes of West Africa (**1**), are dark brown. Others, especially the Hamites (**5**) are light-skinned. The Bantu (**4**) have spread widely south of the Equator. The Bushmen (**2**) were the first inhabitants but were driven into the deserts by the Bantu. The Hottentots (**3**) greeted the first whites to arrive in South Africa.

1

▲ A trumpet used by the Mwembo people as a warning.

▲ A Niam-Niam harpist, in festival dress.

▲ The lyre, the world's oldest instrument, is still played in Africa. Many young musicians are switching to its modern counterpart, the guitar.

## Many races, many gods

The first European explorers took back news of life inside Africa. Sometimes they exaggerated the dangers they suffered, to make themselves seem more brave. Slowly, like a jigsaw, they began to build a picture of how people lived in the world's second biggest continent. All the old tales about strange animals with two heads, about dwarfs and boiling seas along the coastline, were tossed aside. It became understood that Africa was made up of thousands of tribes, some as big as European nations, and some very small. The continent had hundreds of languages. It also possessed many different styles of art and music.

Some of the earliest African cultures were influenced by the civilization of Ancient Egypt. Trading expeditions went down into the Sudan, and from there the secret of iron smelting spread throughout Africa. Then there were the Roman expeditions across the Sahara to the Niger and along the eastern coastline. Such contacts spread new ideas.

But to a great extent, African cultures developed on their own. Empires grew up in West Africa long before the whites arrived there: some of the names, such as Mali and Ghana, have survived. In what is now Rhodesia, the stone-built citadel of Zimbabwe was founded 1,500 years ago. (*See page 43*).

For a long time, it was normal to look down upon the African way of life. For one thing, there were no African written languages, except for the very old Cushite hieroglyphs (which are still undeciphered). Also, the Africans had many religions with ceremonies the Christians did not understand. The Europeans failed to see that there was, in African village life, a balance with nature. People had time to enjoy life, to sing and dance and make carvings, when they were not looking after their crops and animals.

Today the world has learnt to admire African art. The Africans themselves know that they must protect the traditions that were so poorly understood by the first white travellers and merge them with modern styles of life.

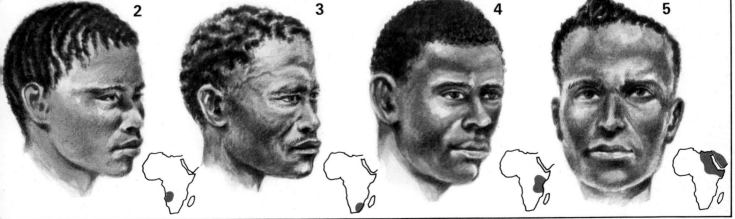

# The Slave Trade in West Africa

▼ **Slave being branded with a trader's initials,** and a branding iron. If the slave escaped, he could then be identified by search parties sent after him. Branding was done in depots on the African coast before the slave ships set out across the Atlantic.

**The Great Triangle** and other slave trade routes

[Map showing: NORTH AMERICA, Southern States, Caribbean Sea, BRAZIL, Pernambuco, Rio de Janeiro, Britain, Holland, EUROPE, AFRICA, Slave Coast, ANGOLA, with routes marked 1, 2, 3]

### The Great Triangle
**1** Cloth, muskets, gin and trinkets taken to Africa for buying slaves.
**2** "Middle passage" took up to four months. Over half the slaves died.
**3** Slave ships sailed home with sugar, rum, cotton and wood.

**Angola Slave Trade.** Angola was called the "Black Mother of Brazil". Trade went on until 1850.

**East Coast Slave Trade.** Fast sailing ships took slaves from East Africa to the Southern States until the American Civil War, 1861.

Areas the slaves were drawn from.

▼ **Below decks on a slave ship,** captives had little room to move. Food was poor, and the air so foul that a candle would not stay alight. In calm weather, sickly slaves were brought on deck and made to dance.

## Black cargoes

Slaves were taken across the Atlantic for more than 300 years—to the West Indies, Brazil and the United States. Nobody can say exactly how many Africans were enslaved. Perhaps 20 million, but many died on the long sea voyage in crowded ships. By 1817, there were two million slaves in Brazil alone. On the American continent today there are 40 million people of Negro blood: they are all descendants of slaves.

Slavery was not a new idea for African chiefs and their subjects. Prisoners taken in wars with other tribes would be treated as slaves—although often they could buy their freedom after a few years. Also, the Arabs practised slavery and took Negro captives across the Sahara for many centuries. But the slavery organized by the Europeans was much bigger in scale and more harmful to African life.

The Europeans needed slaves for their new colonies in America from the 16th century onwards. The plantation owners could do as they liked with the slaves, who were private property. Treatment was usually harsh, and a slave had an average life of seven years in captivity before he died. Women slaves were used as house servants, although some worked in the fields with the men. There were slave mutinies; the leaders were often executed.

By the middle of the 18th century, British ships dominated the Atlantic. In 1785, half the slave ships were British; even in 1807, the year before Britain banned the trade, the port of Liverpool sent to Africa 185 ships, which carried 50,000 slaves.

William Wilberforce, a Member of the British Parliament, was a leader of the campaign to outlaw the "traffic in human beings". It was a long struggle, and in 1833, the West Indian plantation owners were paid £20 million to free their slaves.

The trade across the Atlantic did not end entirely until after 1850: workers were needed for Brazil's coffee plantations, so "pirates" dodged naval patrols along the African coast—to make big profits from their illegal cargoes.

▼ **Bishop Crowther,** a freed slave, was educated in Britain. He returned to West Africa to work as a missionary.

▲ **Before ships raised anchor,** slaves often made a suicide or escape bid. Most were shot, or drowned.

### Slave Trade Debate

**In 1806, the following Resolution** was tabled in the British Parliament: "That conceiving the Slave Trade to be contrary to the principles of justice, humanity and sound policy, this House will, with all practical expedition, take measures to abolish it."

**The resolution was passed** by the House of Lords and by the Commons.

**Lord Grenville:** "What is the purpose of the African Slave Trade? To seize human beings by force . . . and to carry them away from their friends, their families, and their country."

**Lord Westmorland:** "The Slave Trade is a trade with the consent of the inhabitants of two nations, and procured by no terror, or any act of violence whatever."

**Mr William Wilberforce:** "If one thousandth part of the real horrors of this traffic were to be the subject of actual vision with those its defenders, none of their arguments, I am confident, would be argued again."

**General Tarleton:** "I have no doubt that much evil will result to this country at large from the abolition of the Slave Trade."

# South Africa's White Settlers

▲ **Dutch farmers** made their own styles of architecture, with high, curving gables. They were great readers of the Bible, believing God had sent them to Africa to civilize it. An English preacher in Cape Province painted this picture.

▲ **Jan van Riebeeck** set up, in 1652, an outpost at the Cape. Seeds from Europe were planted to grow vegetables.

▲ **His wife**, Maria, was 19 when she arrived. Van Riebeeck sent for "lusty farm wenches" from Holland for his men.

◀ **The Flintlock gun** was used by the Dutch settlers for shooting game and Africans— who feared these strangers able to "spit fire". The cow horn was kept filled with gunpowder.

▼ **Hottentots** greeted Van Riebeeck when he stepped ashore. But many of them were wiped out in a smallpox epidemic; few survive today.

▼ **Zulus** fought against the white settlers. Their army was crushed at Blood River in 1838. Africans were living in the Transvaal for 1,000 years before the whites arrived.

▶ **Mountainous country** stood between the Boers and the fertile farmlands north of the Cape. Men and oxen dragged the waggons up rough tracks in the Drakensberg Range, which rises to more than 11,000 ft. The trekkers set up their own republics.

▲ **Voortrekkers resting.** The Boer farmers crossed the Orange River (named after the Dutch Prince of Orange) to get away from the British.

## The Dutch colonists and the Great Trek

On the southern tip of Africa was a small white settlement called Cape Town. The "Cape of Good Hope" had been rounded by Vasco da Gama in 1498, but for 300 years nobody cared much about it.

In 1652 a Dutch surgeon went ashore with his wife and 90 soldiers, following orders of the Dutch East India Company to set up a "refreshment station" for ships. The surgeon was called Jan van Riebeeck. He stayed for ten years, but the colony only began to prosper under the direction of a half-caste named Simon van der Stel.

The strength of the settlement was increased when 150 French Protestants arrived in 1688, fleeing from religious persecution in Europe. These Frenchmen, called Huguenots, started wine-growing. Most of the hard work was done by slaves from Malaya and West Africa. Cape Town's reputation grew very slowly: after more than a century it had only 3,500 people. The Africans living at the Cape were sheep-farmers who called themselves *Khoikhoin*; the Dutch nicknamed them Hottentots in mimicry of their language.

The Whites looked for more land, to the north and east of Cape Town. They were resisted by the *San* people (Bushmen) who fought with poisoned arrows but were no match for the white Boers (farmers) with their firearms. Most of the bushmen were wiped out, the last of them retreating to the Drakensberg Mountains and the Kalahari desert.

The Boers were tough and adventurous. They did not want to be a colony of any European nation. They were bitter when new laws were imposed on them by the British, who occupied Cape Town at the start of the 19th century. One of these laws banned slavery, which the Boers relied upon to run their farms. So in 1835 the Great Trek began. It took the Boers across the Orange River and from there they spread out to start farms all over much of what is now South Africa.

**The Great Trek, 1835**

⟹ Great Trek

Transvaal

Orange Free State

Limpopo R.

Matabele

R. Vaal

Zulus

R. Orange

CAPE COLONY

15

# Trade and the Travellers

▲ **A 1780 Viennese coin**, the "Maria Theresa dollar", used as currency in Ethiopia and East Africa for 100 years.

## Gold across the desert, ivory from the jungle

Long before the European and Arab travellers came to Africa, its peoples had been trading with the outside world. Ships from India and China sailed to Africa with beads, cloth and Chinese porcelain, and exchanged them for ivory, ebony and leopard skins. African craftsmen were smelting copper; the metal was carried to the coast in long bars or crosses, to offer to traders from the Red Sea. In the north, camels crossed the Sahara with silverware, pottery and ornaments, to barter for gold and slaves. These foreign trade goods did in time reach tribes far inland. By 1800, trading posts had been started all around Africa by the Dutch, Portuguese and British; ships collected ivory, wood and hides.

**Trade routes in Africa, 1400–1600**

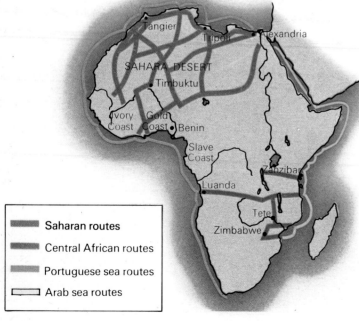

Tangier
Tripoli
Alexandria
SAHARA DESERT
Timbuktu
Ivory Coast
Gold Coast
Benin
Slave Coast
Zanzibar
Luanda
Tete
Zimbabwe

- Saharan routes
- Central African routes
- Portuguese sea routes
- Arab sea routes

## The Story of a Billiard Ball
The African bull elephants were hunted for their tusks.

## Bartering for food

When an explorer set off into the unknown, he could not take along money or cheques to buy food for himself and his followers. He needed to have with him many rolls of cloth, jackets, beads, wire and guns, to exchange for chickens, maize flour and vegetables. African trade worked by barter, and anything could be exchanged—including live animals and people. It was possible to buy a slave with rolls of cloth, and when King Mutesa of Buganda sent some big elephant tusks to the British in Zanzibar he said he wanted in return a white woman and an Indian cook.

In East Africa, a popular trade item was a strong cotton called "Merikani" (American); it was brought all the way from Massachusetts. The chiefs also wanted beads to give to their wives for making necklaces and belts. But a traveller had to be very careful to know what kinds of goods were popular in the lands he intended to visit. Otherwise he might find that his loads of beads would not buy enough food to save the expedition from starvation.

In West Africa, traders supplied alcohol to the chiefs to win their friendship. So strong drink became a "currency". Men demanded it as wages for working as porters. This is why the claim is sometimes made that Europeans came to Africa with a bottle of gin in one hand and the Bible in the other.

▲ **Explorers bargaining for food** with cloth, shells and beads. When an expedition halted in the forest, two shots were fired in the air to signal to local people to come and barter.

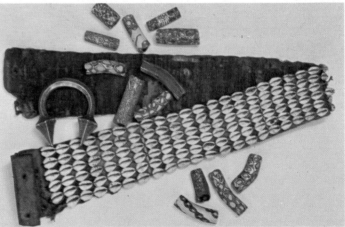

▲ **Currencies in Africa.** A silver "manilla", beads and a belt of cowrie shells: they were used instead of money.

The bodies supplied meat, but the big prize was the ivory.

Porters trekked to the coast where traders and ships were waiting.

In Europe, the tusks were turned into billiard balls and piano keys.

# Livingstone — the Early Years

◀ **David Livingstone.** Born in Blantyre, Scotland in 1813, Livingstone began work at the age of ten in a mill. The hours were from six in the morning until eight at night, with half a day off a week. But evening school after work gave him the chance to learn Latin, science and mathematics. By saving up his pay, he was able at the age of 23 to train as a doctor. In November 1840 he was ordained and sailed for Africa as a missionary.

◀▲ **The Victoria Falls.** By becoming the first white man to cross Africa (1853-6), Livingstone suddenly won fame. On the way he was taken in a Barotse canoe to see the world's greatest waterfall, a mile wide and 300 ft. high. The Africans called it *Mosi-o-Tunya* ("the Smoke that Thunders"), but he decided to honour the British Queen by calling it Victoria Falls. These paintings were made by Thomas Baines four years later.

### Livingstone in Africa

In 1850, Livingstone took his family with him into the Kalahari Desert. They nearly died of thirst, but reached Lake Ngami.

Livingstone quarrelled with the Boers over their treatment of Africans. In 1852 they burnt down his house at Kolobeng.

While 1,000 warriors looked on, Livingstone conferred with the powerful chief Shinte in his capital near the Zambezi.

## Livingstone's Journeys 1841–63

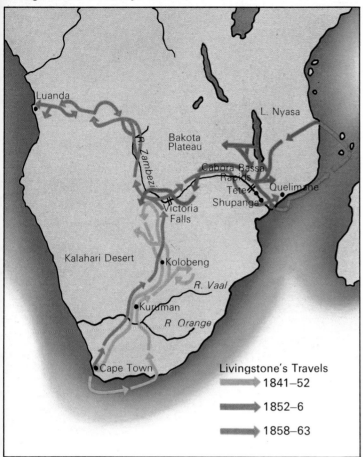

Luanda
L. Nyasa
Bakota Plateau
R. Zambezi
Cabora Bassa Rapids
Tete
Quelimane
Shupanga
Victoria Falls
Kalahari Desert
Kolobeng
R. Vaal
Kuruman
R. Orange
Cape Town

**Livingstone's Travels**
→ 1841–52
→ 1852–6
→ 1858–63

David Livingstone led the way in Central Africa for the white pioneers. A hundred years ago he was a great hero in Britain: every child was told to be like him—brave, kind to the weak and poor, and never admitting defeat. Gradually, this view of Livingstone has changed somewhat. He neglected his own family and he was harsh to his white companions.

He began in the south, where he worked as a missionary for eight years. But by 1850 his ambition was to explore the Zambezi region. Livingstone sent his wife and children back to Britain as they were hampering his travels. Then in 1852 he began the journey that excited all Europe. By 1856, Livingstone had travelled from the Upper Zambezi to the Atlantic, then back eastwards to the Indian Ocean.

He returned to Britain, but was eager to go back to Africa, and recruited six white assistants. He had been made a "roving consul" by the Government and would sail up the Zambezi and develop trade with the interior, as well as setting up Christian missions. But Livingstone had made one terrible mistake—although he had seen one huge waterfall, and named it after Queen Victoria, he had missed the Cabora Bassa rapids. Later he realized that these made it impossible to turn the river into "God's highway"

This was just the first blow for the expedition. Livingstone pinned many hopes on his paddle steamer (below) but it proved slow and leaky. It was called *Ma-Robert*—the African name for Mrs Livingstone, whose eldest son was Robert. Mrs Livingstone joined the expedition on the Zambezi in early 1862, but died of malaria at Shupanga. Beset by sorrow and worries, Livingstone kept the expedition going until 1864, and did manage to explore Lake Nyasa. He sadly returned home. But in time, he would go yet again to Africa.

▲ **Livingstone's travels** began in South Africa and took him to the unknown forests north of the Zambezi. Arab traders were wandering across the continent, and the Portuguese knew something of the interior, but Livingstone was the first man to give to the world maps and scientific information about it. His discoveries drew missionaries and traders to Central Africa—and many died while following his footsteps.

On the Zambezi, a female hippopotamus that had lost its young attacked Livingstone's canoe, throwing the paddlers into the river.

Slavery in Africa was run by Arabs and Portuguese half-castes, bartering guns for people. Livingstone sketched the caravans.

On his 1852–56 journey, he travelled alone. When he returned to Africa with white aides and this steamboat, he achieved less.

Black preacher
with two pygmies

Roman Catholic
White Fathers

A native wedding in Barotseland

The wife of a missionary
teaching a group of women in Uganda.

An early Methodist missionary party

◄ **On the opposite page** is a collection of original photographs of Christian missionaries during the last century in Africa.

# Muslims and Christians

The African peoples have always had their own religions. They worshipped the things around them: waterfalls and mountains were often believed to be the places where sacred spirits lived. But the strangers from Asia and Europe offered new religions—Islam (the Muslim faith) and Christianity. These two faiths, both started in the Middle East, have long been rivals in Africa; eagerness to spread them and win converts inspired great journeys by Arabs and Christians.

Many Christian travellers died from malaria or through being ambushed in the forests. But the missionaries did succeed in some parts of Africa. Today there are African bishops and preachers over much of the continent. Also, the Africans have founded new Christian sects, with their own preachers, churches, hymns and types of service. They have been encouraged to do this by seeing that Europeans themselves have different kinds of Christianity. These "many faces" of Christianity have tended to make Africans turn away from it.

This has not happened with Islam, which is growing steadily. Moreover, the Islamic Holy book, the Koran, does not condemn African traditions, such as having more than one wife. Islam was spread throughout the lands along the southern edge of the Sahara by wandering Arab merchants after A.D. 800. They started towns, such as Timbuktu, which became centres of learning. But they did not try to impose the new religion on the chiefs, many of whom were treated as gods by their subjects.

Sometimes Islam was spread by invading armies, engaged in a *jihad*, or holy war. In A.D. 1076 the ancient state of Ghana was conquered by the Almoravids, fanatical warriors from the north. Eight hundred years later the last great Muslim invasion in West Africa took place under Othman dan Fodio. He aroused all the Fulani tribes to conquer much of what is now Nigeria. They went into battle holding green banners embroidered with texts from the Koran. They fought with great bravery: the Prophet, Mohammed, promised that a man who died in battle would go straight to heaven.

One of the best-known Islamic uprisings was in the Sudan 100 years ago. A religious leader calling himself the Madhi, a new prophet, declared he would "abolish the tyranny of the rich" and collected an army of 300,000. Efforts to stop him were unsuccessful and in January 1885 he captured Khartoum, where the British General Charles Gordon was besieged. Eventually the Madhi's troops were destroyed by General Kitchener. Today, Africa has 80 million Muslims and 50 million Christians. In Zambia, there is a town named after David Livingstone.

▲ **A Muslim mosque** made of sun-dried bricks at Timbuktu in Mali. After A.D. 600, the Islamic armies swept along to the Atlantic and down to West Africa.

► **Coptic crosses** are carried by priests in Ethiopia, which was converted to Christianity in A.D. 350.

▼ There was a legend in Europe that a Christian king, **Prester John,** was surrounded by hostile tribes in the heart of Africa.

# The Nile Mystery

▼ **Richard Burton,** leader of the first Nile expedition. His scar was from a spear-wound.

▼ **James Grant,** a tall Scot, wrote *A Walk Across Africa* about his two-year trip.

The Ancient Egyptians believed that the Nile "flowed from the beginning of the world." But the cause of the river's yearly flooding, rising in July and falling in September, was a mystery to them. The Greek geographer Ptolemy knew the Nile began south of the Equator in a series of lakes, and the Arabs were able to describe the snow-covered "Mountains of the Moon", from which many streams cascaded into the great river.

This was all that the rest of the world knew about the Great Lakes region of Africa until 1850. Then two German Protestant missionaries, Krapf and Rebmann, began exploring from Mombasa. They heard reports from Zanzibari slavers of a huge lake inland called Ujiji, and drew a crude map of it. This was sent to the Royal Geographical Society in London and caused a sensation. The hunt for the source of the Nile was on.

The R.G.S. invited Captain Richard Burton of the Indian Army to mount an expedition to find the "Sea of Ujiji". As his companion he chose another army officer, John Speke; in 1857 they started off from Bagamoyo. By November they reached Tabora, 500 miles inland, and there gained the first accurate information about the "Sea of Ujiji". In fact, Ujiji was a town on Lake Tanganyika, which was quite separate from Lake Nyasa, further south; there were more lakes in the north. Three months later they reached Lake Tanganyika and explored part of it in a *dhow* (an Arab sailing boat.) On the way back to the coast, while Burton was lying sick, Speke made a quick trip to Lake Victoria.

Speke at once claimed that he had discovered the true source of the Nile, since the lake was more than 3,700 ft above sea level. Bitter jealousy between him and Burton developed, and for the next 15 years the controversy about the "Sources" was raging. Speke was sent back by the R.G.S. to Africa with another army colleague, James Grant, to make good his claims. The British Government backed the journey financially, as it had backed Burton and Speke.

Slow progress was made by Speke and Grant. Their porters deserted, most of the African chiefs they met were unco-operative and both men fell seriously ill. But they reached Lake Victoria by way of Tabora, and finally on July 28, 1862, Speke saw the Ripon Falls, where the Nile leaves the lake. This was eventually to be accepted as the main source of the river, but Speke was challenged because he had not traced it northwards from the falls. Samuel Baker soon afterwards found Lake Albert and put forward his claim. Later David Livingstone was to offer other theories, which proved completely wrong. Speke did not live to see his case proved. Just before he was to have a public debate with Burton, he shot himself.

▲ **John Speke** first travelled with Burton in Somaliland, where they were both wounded. In August 1858 he saw Africa's greatest lake, and named it Victoria.

▼ **On his second African expedition,** Speke travelled around Lake Victoria. He shot three white rhinos, and gave the heads to a chief as a goodwill gesture.

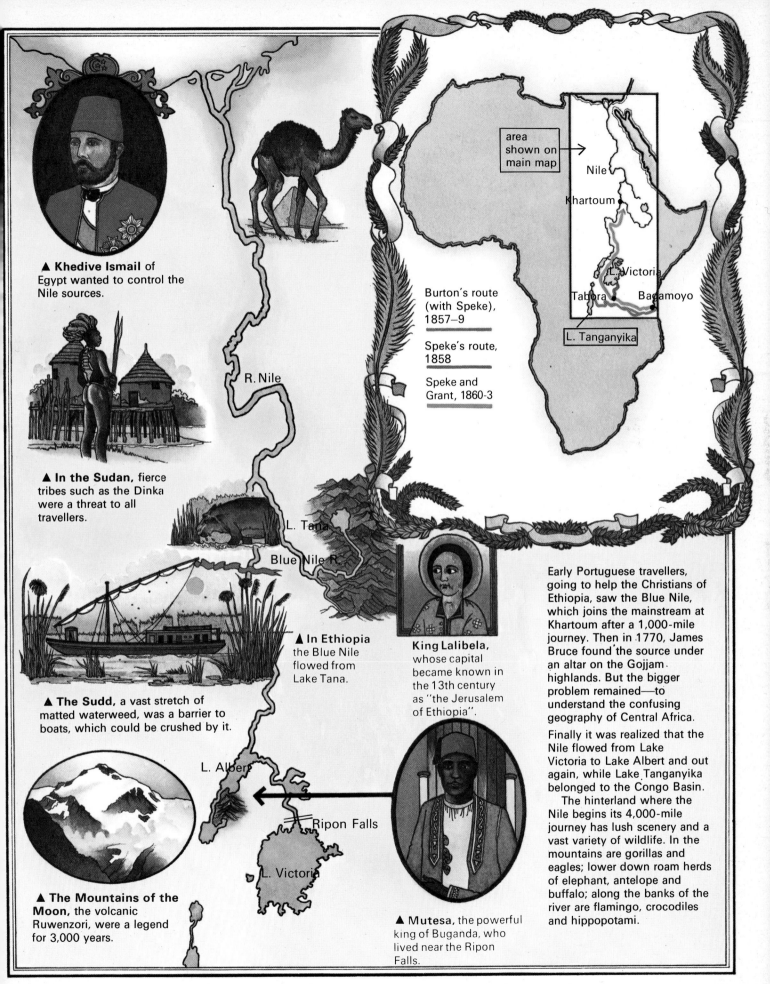

▲ **Khedive Ismail** of Egypt wanted to control the Nile sources.

▲ **In the Sudan,** fierce tribes such as the Dinka were a threat to all travellers.

▲ **The Sudd,** a vast stretch of matted waterweed, was a barrier to boats, which could be crushed by it.

▲ **The Mountains of the Moon,** the volcanic Ruwenzori, were a legend for 3,000 years.

R. Nile

L. Tana

Blue Nile R.

▲ **In Ethiopia** the Blue Nile flowed from Lake Tana.

**King Lalibela,** whose capital became known in the 13th century as "the Jerusalem of Ethiopia".

L. Albert

Ripon Falls

L. Victoria

▲ **Mutesa,** the powerful king of Buganda, who lived near the Ripon Falls.

area shown on main map

Nile

Khartoum

L. Victoria

Tabora          Bagamoyo

L. Tanganyika

Burton's route (with Speke), 1857–9

Speke's route, 1858

Speke and Grant, 1860-3

Early Portuguese travellers, going to help the Christians of Ethiopia, saw the Blue Nile, which joins the mainstream at Khartoum after a 1,000-mile journey. Then in 1770, James Bruce found the source under an altar on the Gojjam highlands. But the bigger problem remained—to understand the confusing geography of Central Africa.

Finally it was realized that the Nile flowed from Lake Victoria to Lake Albert and out again, while Lake Tanganyika belonged to the Congo Basin.
   The hinterland where the Nile begins its 4,000-mile journey has lush scenery and a vast variety of wildlife. In the mountains are gorillas and eagles; lower down roam herds of elephant, antelope and buffalo; along the banks of the river are flamingo, crocodiles and hippopotami.

# Samuel and Florence Baker

▶ **Lady Baker and Sir Samuel Baker.** When she reached London in 1865 after their travels, Florence won fame as the first woman explorer of Central Africa. Her husband praised her coolness in the face of danger. "She was not a screamer," he said proudly. With his favourite hunting rifle, Sir Samuel poses in his *safari* outfit.

▶ **At the Murchison Falls** the Nile drops 130 ft. and enters Lake Albert. The Bakers were the first Europeans to see the waterfall. They sailed on the lake in an effort to explore it and were caught in a storm which almost drowned them. Baker thought he had found the true source of the Nile, but later explorations proved that the river flows from Lake Victoria to Lake Albert.

▼ **Baker** was untrained in painting, but enjoyed trying to record in watercolours exciting moments of his travels.

▲ **After Baker had shot** a buffalo, it charged and killed Sali Achmet, an Egyptian servant; it then fell dead.

▼ **A funeral:** "The dancers were most grotesquely got up . . . huge ostrich feathers adorned their helmets."

▲ **Chased by a rhino:** "We heard the sharp whistling snort, and a tremendous rush through the high grass . . ."

▼ **Welcome home:** "The native women crowded in . . . to dance in honour of our return."

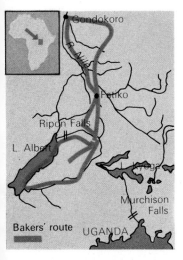

Bakers' route  UGANDA

## The Bakers and the Nile

Samuel and Florence Baker were unusual people who met in an unusual way. He was travelling in a part of eastern Europe then under Turkish rule, and saw a girl being auctioned off in a market. A rich Turk was about to buy her when Sam Baker stepped in and offered more money. The future Lady Baker was 18, Hungarian and blonde, and her purchaser was an English hunting enthusiast nearly twice her age. Together they set off for Africa, where Baker decided to join in the fashionable adventure of looking for the Nile Sources.

At the end of 1862 their expedition left Khartoum in three boats. Baker had nearly 100 followers, as well as camels, horses and donkeys. Apart from Florence, there was one other white companion—a young German named Schmidt. The boats took the expedition 1,000 miles south from Khartoum to Gondokoro. On the way, Schmidt died of malaria. Then the Bakers met Speke and Grant, who were on their way home to Britain after visiting Uganda. It looked to Baker as though he had been beaten in the search, since Speke was convinced that his discovery of the Ripon Falls settled the "Nile mystery" once and for all. But when Speke revealed there was a big, unexplored lake to the south-west, the Bakers decided to look for it.

The next year tested the courage of Sam and Florence to the utmost. They were caught in tribal wars, their own men mutinied, and food ran short. Once Florence was delirious for a week and in all that time Sam sat by her without sleeping. On another occasion a chief named Kamrasi wanted to take Florence into his harem. But at last the Bakers reached the mysterious lake, which they named Albert after Queen Victoria's husband. Once back in London, the Bakers were married, amid a tumult of hero-worship. Sir Samuel's account of their adventures, *The Albert Nyanza*, became a classic of African travel.

Several years later the Bakers returned to the Upper Nile, to administer the Sudan for Egypt. They lived in style in Khartoum, taking with them expensive wines and fine china and crystal. In an effort to extend Egyptian rule to Lake Victoria, Baker fought his way down to the capital of Kabba Rega, son of the chief who had tried to buy Florence ten years earlier. After a pitched battle, Baker's expedition retreated, harassed day and night by Kabba Rega's spearmen.

Before he left the Sudan for good, Baker Pasha—as the Khedive Ismail called him—managed to establish a fort at Fatiko, just north of Lake Victoria. He was succeeded by General Charles Gordon, who strengthened Egyptian rule but finally was surrounded and killed in Khartoum by the Mahdists. After Baker retired from Egyptian service he did not return to Africa. Until his death in 1893 he was a mainstay of the Royal Geographical Society.

▲ **Attacked by an elephant:** "An immense fellow with tusks about five feet long . . . He charged straight into me."

▼ **Life in the wilds.** The explorers take a morning stroll. In the foreground is Lady Baker's pet monkey, Wallady.

# An Explorer's Kit

▶ **Double-roof ridge tent.** The first aim of the explorer after his day's journey was to pitch his tent. It had to be strongly made to stand up to tropical storms. In the evenings, by the light of a candle or hurricane lamp, he would sit in his tent to write up his travel diary.

**Solar topee.** Today, few people in Africa wear topees. But a century ago, white travellers were afraid of so-called sunstroke. Many wore felt spine pads against the sun.

▼ **Rifles and shotguns.** An expedition would depend for survival on its guns. The explorer had to kill wild animals for meat; sometimes lions and leopards were shot in self-defence. Battles developed with tribes who were suspicious of the strangers marching through their lands. Guns were also useful to give as presents to chiefs. Many of the explorers were army officers, who took with them a huge armoury of weapons.

Big game gun

Single-barrel, smooth bore gun

Ammunition box

**Belt and bags** to hold small tools, whistles, knives and ammunition.

▼ **Tools and ropes.** In the African interior, paths often had to be made through the forests, so axes and machetes were essential to any explorer. He also needed ropes for dragging equipment up steep cliffs, and knives for skinning animals. Spades were used for making defences around the camp—and for digging the graves of men who died.

◀ **Medicine chest,** as advertised in a catalogue of 1907. Big expeditions took a doctor along, but most relied upon a carefully-prepared medicine chest. It held quinine for treating malaria, splints and bandages, ointments for stings and rashes caused by poisonous plants, and an assortment of pills.

▲ **Magic lantern,** which caused amazement in the middle of Africa. Missionary travellers gave "picture shows" to win converts. Light was provided by a candle.

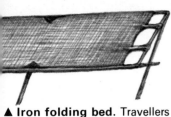

▲ **Iron folding bed.** Travellers trying to adapt to African life slept on the ground, on straw mats. Some did not like this, and brought along folding beds, which the porters carried on their heads. Another luxury was a carpet, unfolded every evening to cover the ground inside the tent.

▼ **Combined table and desk,** said to have been used by Livingstone. A folding stool with a canvas seat, and a light table for writing on, were all the pieces of furniture that the average explorer wanted.

**Knee boots** protected the legs in swamps and kept out mosquitoes and insects.

▶ **Oppewill sliding box camera** and developing fluids. By the middle of the last century, photography was just beginning. The equipment was heavy and slow, and the pictures, taken on glass plates, often broke.

▼ **African gourds,** used for carrying water. Canvas bags were also used. In desert regions, many explorers died from thirst under the hot sun. In the jungles, it was dangerous to drink water from pools and slow-running rivers, for fear of dysentery and other diseases. Wise explorers always boiled their drinking water.

# What the explorers took with them

When a traveller swallowed something he feared was poisonous, he knew exactly what to do: "Drink a charge of gunpowder in a tumblerful of warm water and tickle the throat." This recipe for making yourself sick was given in *The Art of Travel, or, Shifts and Contrivances Available in Wild Countries*, by Francis Galton. First published in 1854, Galton's book was the bible of would-be explorers for 40 years. It was based on his own experiences as an African traveller, and started off cheerfully: "Savages rarely murder newcomers; they fear their guns, and have a superstitious awe of the white man's power." Galton's list of essentials ranged from butcher's knives to books to read in camp at night.

The clothes explorers wore varied greatly, according to their personal whims. A solar topee (*see picture, left*) was the normal headgear, but some travellers chose straw hats with veils to keep off the insects. It was thought vital to wear flannel next to the skin, regardless of the climate, and long woollen socks— the hotter the ground, the thicker the socks.

One traveller who marched across Africa, Dr James Johnston, took a cornet with him and played tunes such as *Way Down Upon the Swanee River* to the chiefs when they seemed threatening. He claimed it saved his life. Other explorers used firework displays to get them out of risky situations.

Animals taken to carry supplies rarely survived long expeditions. The advantage of oxen was that they could carry 120 lb. (twice as much as a donkey's load) and gave rations for 80 men for a day when slaughtered. A camel could bear the greatest load— 300 lb.—but was only useful in desert regions.

All white explorers relied heavily upon the skills of their African "expedition captains". Some of the Zanzibari guides were as famous, 100 years ago, as the *Sherpas* who help mountaineers in the Himalayas.

▼ **Boat built in sections** so that it could be carried overland. Stanley made his historic journey down the Congo River in the *Lady Alice* after it had been carried 5,000 miles from Zanzibar.

# The Death of Livingstone

▲ **Agnes** was Livingstone's favourite among his children. He wrote her long, loving letters from the heart of Africa.

▼ **Livingstone** spent years searching for the source of the Nile. In April 1873 he was too sick and weak to walk, or even to ride a donkey. His followers made a litter and carried him through the swamps beside Lake Bangweulu. To the last he made geographical notes in his diary. He died praying.

▼ **His last request** (May 1, 1873) was for this medicine bottle.

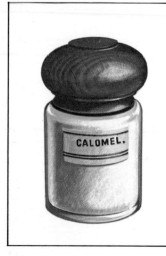

CALOMEL.

◄ **Susi and Chuma**, two Africans who stayed with Livingstone throughout his last journey, were brought to Britain after his death. Chuma was a freed slave; both he and Susi came from what is now Malawi. With relics of the explorer they posed for a photographer in 1874 at Newstead Abbey, near Nottingham. The assembled relics include the Union Jack put over Livingstone's coffin, his Riley double-barrelled rifle, consular sword and cap, Bible, maps, journals and notebooks.

**Henry Stanley** was the only white man to see Livingstone on his last journey (March 1866 – May 1873). An adventurer who had fought on both sides in the American Civil War, Stanley made a 700-mile trek to Ujiji from Zanzibar. His two white companions died on the way. The greeting, "Dr Livingstone, I presume?" became the most famous phrase in the history of African travel. Livingstone refused to return home, and Stanley left him after four months.

**Furthermost point** reached by Livingstone on his last journey was the Lualaba River, main tributary of the Congo. But most of his followers deserted him, so he relied on Arabs for aid.

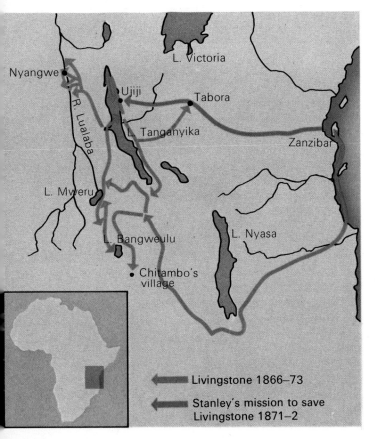

➡ Livingstone 1866–73

⬅ Stanley's mission to save Livingstone 1871–2

## Livingstone's last journey

When Livingstone left England for the last time in 1865, he was an unhappy, disappointed man. His previous expedition, to the Zambezi River and Lake Nyasa, had been a failure, costing the lives of his wife and several companions. The British Government was cold towards his ideas for further explorations in Central Africa.

But Africa drew him back. The Royal Geographical Society asked him to solve the puzzle about the Nile watershed. He was more than 50 and in failing health, but he was determined to make one more great discovery and so to restore his reputation. Livingstone raised £2,000 to equip himself—half of it given by a Glasgow merchant. His journey took seven years. It ended with his death in May 1873 at the village of Chitambo, in what is now Zambia.

As the old traveller wandered about in the forests to the south and west of Lake Tanganyika, the world almost forgot him. But friends in London were anxious at reports of his death. A search party went out, which failed to find Livingstone, but confirmed that he was still living. Occasionally letters from him reached the coast at Zanzibar; the British consulate there sent supplies into the interior for him, although most of them were stolen.

Then in 1872 came the news that a young journalist, Henry Stanley, had met Livingstone at Ujiji. Stanley was working for the *New York Herald*, but he was Welsh and his real name was John Rowlands. His arrival at Ujiji coincided with Livingstone's retreat from the Lualaba River, where he had seen a massacre of 400 African villagers by Arab brigands. By now the old explorer was short of supplies, and half dead; only a small band of African "faithfuls" were still with him.

The food and companionship of Stanley gave Livingstone a new surge of life. They parted after four months—Stanley to bring back his great scoop and write his bestseller, *How I Found Livingstone*, and the missionary to go on wandering. He died going south, looking for the mythical "fountains of Herodotus" he thought would prove to be the true source of the Nile. His followers buried his heart under a tree, dried his body in the sun, then carried it, wrapped in sailcloth and matting, to the coast. Livingstone was buried, with great emotion and ceremony, in Westminster Abbey in London.

In his last seven years, Livingstone discovered little. His ideas about the source of the Nile were soon proved wrong. But many good things were to be done in his name, including a stepping up of the campaign against the slave trade in the African interior. He led the "civilizing mission" of white men in Africa. This "mission" was also to be the excuse, ten years after his death, for the carve-up of Africa into colonies.

# Scientific Explorers

▲ **Heinrich Barth,** a German geographer, spent five years around the Sahara, making precise accounts of his travels.

▲ **Georg Schweinfurth** was the first white man to see a pygmy. He was also a tireless collector of plants.

▲ **The Emperor Swallowtail,** one of the biggest of Africa's 2,400 species of butterflies. Its wingspan can be nearly 6 ins. Butterfly collectors found West Africa's jungles to contain more varieties than anywhere else.

## Scientists in Africa

After 1850, following the early explorers, the interest of scientists turned to tropical Africa. Museums, universities and learned societies all over Europe sent men into the heart of the continent to look for rare plants, insects, birds and animals. The travellers took with them delicate instruments; these had to be carried over rough paths by African porters, who might slip in the mud or trip over tree roots.

The traveller Francis Galton gave advice to would-be explorers on how to look after scientific equipment. He said it was best to pick an old man to be the porter, because "his infirmities compelled him to walk steadily". A box of instruments would not be as heavy as a load of cloth or rope, so the old man "would be delighted at the prospect of picking up a living by such easy service."

Apart from his sextant, chronometer and compass, the explorer took along boxes in which to store his beetles and butterflies, and tweezers for gently holding these specimens. Cameras were likely to be ruined by dampness and dust, so they had to be wrapped in waterproof cloth. The careful scientific traveller made records every day about his geographical surveys, and the details of temperature and rainfall. In his early years as an explorer, Livingstone was reprimanded by the Royal Geographical Society for not keeping proper records.

Not all the explorers were experts in the fields for which they are remembered. A French adventurer, Paul du Chaillu, caused a sensation among scientists when he became the first white man to capture a gorilla. Many people would not believe it existed.

▲ **Giant groundsel** on Mount Elgon in East Africa. The climax of exploration came at the same time as a growth of interest in natural history. Travellers in Africa were urged to bring back botanical specimens for museums.

▼ **Wild boar and reitbok antelope,** by the naturalist, Cornwallis-Harris. In 1859, Darwin published his *Origin of the Species*, on the relationship of man to the animals. Explorers went to Africa in excitement at what they might find

◀ **King Manza** as seen by Schweinfurth in March 1870, when he visited the Monbuttoo country. The artist carefully noted the ruler's hat of plaited reeds, adorned with three layers of parrot feathers, and the bars of copper he wore through his pierced ears.

▶ **A Loobah woman** with a circular plate of ivory in her upper lip and a cone of quartz through her lower lip. Schweinfurth described how the women had to raise their upper lips to drink. While exploring, he made hundreds of exact drawings like this one.

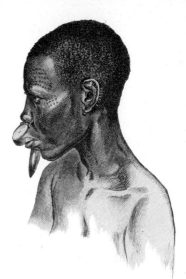

◀▼ **David Livingstone used the sextant** (left) during his journey across Africa. The picture below shows how it was held. A sextant has an arc or circle marked in degrees, and has a mirror that reflects light from a star or the sun onto a silvered glass. By adjusting the angles of the glass, the star appears to rest on the horizon. The angle is then read and checked against astronomical tables to give the explorer's position.

▼ **A compass** was the basic equipment for plotting a route and making maps. In thick, high jungle an expedition would go in circles without a compass.

▼ One man's job was to measure the daily march with a "**waywiser**". The number of times the wheel went around was multiplied by its circumference.

▼ **A minerologist** examines a rock. Many explorers began as prospectors: Joseph Thomson was sent by the Sultan of Zanzibar to look for coal and was sacked for not finding any.

▼ **Boiling a thermometer** to discover the altitude. The higher the altitude, the lower the boiling point—this was a method used by explorers who had lost their instruments.

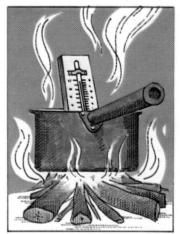

# Stanley—from Zanzibar to Banana Point

Until the 1870's, no white traveller had managed to cross Africa along the line of the Equator. The Congo River poured into the Atlantic Ocean at Banana Point, on the west coast, and it was obviously one of the biggest rivers in the world. Yet its course in the interior was a mystery: only a short way inland the river cascaded over foaming rapids which stopped all expeditions by boat. The hot, unhealthy climate discouraged overland journeys.

The man who decided to crack this puzzle was Henry Stanley, the young journalist who found Livingstone in 1871. He did it partly through love of adventure, but also out of anger—some people in Britain called him a hoaxer. He wrote: "I will compel those who doubt I discovered Livingstone at Ujiji to confess themselves in error." So he set off from Zanzibar in 1874 with 350 Africans and three young Englishmen. One was a London hotel clerk named Frederick Barker; Frank and Edward Pocock were sons of a Kentish fisherman. The aim was to map Lake Victoria, visited by Speke and Grant ten years before, go on to Lake Tanganyika, then march westwards towards the Lualaba river—which Livingstone had imagined was one of the sources of the Nile. Stanley rightly guessed it was a main tributary of the Congo.

Stanley did all he set out to do: after 999 days he reached the mouth of the Congo after a desperate journey down the river. But the cost was terrible. Only 130 of his followers were still alive; his white assistants were all dead. Troubles began early. Just before Christmas 1874, Stanley sent a letter to his American girl-friend, Alice Pike: "There is a famine . . . I have not eaten a piece of meat for ten days . . . Three of my dogs are dead . . . One of my donkeys was killed last night by a hyena." One of the casualties of the journey was Kalulu, a former child slave who was Stanley's adopted son. He and Frank Pocock were drowned in the Congo rapids. The struggle made Stanley grey-haired at the age of 35.

Although he was now world-famous and his triumph silenced all his enemies, Stanley suffered a personal disappointment: his journey took so long that his girl-friend married somebody else. So he went back to the Congo in 1879 as an employee of King Leopold II of the Belgians, and worked there for five years, doing more exploring and opening up trading stations. His efforts were rivalled by France's best known African explorer, Count Savorgnan de Brazza, who was attempting to carve out a colony for his country in the Congo basin. But Stanley's explorations in the Congo region gave Belgium the biggest colony in Africa, covering nearly one million square miles.

▲ **1** With flags flying, Stanley set off from Zanzibar and marched across Africa. Here he leads the way towards Lake Albert, first discovered by Samuel and Florence Baker. But hostile warriors forced him to retreat and head southwards.

▲ **4** To sail down the Congo, Stanley's expedition used a flotilla of canoes. At the front was the *Lady Alice*, which had to be carried in sections until the river was reached. Near the Atlantic it was abandoned.

▼ **The expedition** covered 7,100 miles. The most exciting part was the last nine months, following the Congo in its double crossing of the Equator.

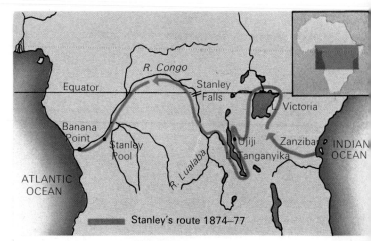

Stanley's route 1874–77

▲ **2** Warfare and illness soon cut down his followers. One of the first to die was Edward Pocock. Here, Stanley reads the burial service while Edward's brother kneels in prayer with Frederick Barker—who died soon after.

▲ **3** Stanley forced his way across Africa by using the latest weapons. Near the Lualaba River he met a powerful slave-trader, Tippu Tib. To impress him he gave a rapid-fire demonstration with his repeating rifle.

▲ **5** Fighting all the way. The people living along the river were suspicious of the strangers travelling downstream. They attacked in canoes sometimes holding 100 warriors in each. Stanley came through 30 battles.

▲ **6** Journey's end. At the small port of Boma, near Banana Point, Stanley was welcomed by European traders. In the background are the expedition's Zanzibari "captains".

▼ **Stanley** in uniform. The Africans called him *Bula Matari*—"Smasher of Rocks".

▼ **Tippu Tib** controlled much of Central Africa. Eventually, the Arabs were driven out.

▼ **Count de Brazza,** seen in Arab disguise, won part of the Congo for France.

▼ **Leopold II** hired Stanley. He argued, "Belgium must have a colony"—and took the Congo.

# Women Travellers

▲ **Mary Kingsley** from Cambridge explored the Ogowé River in the Congo. She went to Africa in 1892 as a trader and amateur anthropologist. She died in South Africa.

▲ **Alexandrine Tinné,** a rich young Dutchwoman, went up the Nile in 1861 with her mother and her aunt. When they died, she continued alone. Tuaregs killed her in 1869.

▼ **May French Sheldon** was an American who in 1891 dared to enter the Masai country. She was the first white woman to reach Mt. Kilimanjaro. Below: the wickerwork palanquin in which she slept and was carried.

▲ **Katherine Petherick** travelled in unknown country west of the Upper Nile in 1862 with her husband.

## Women in the "white man's grave"

In the heyday of African exploration the perils were thought too great for the "gentler sex". But Lady Baker (*see pages 24–5*) endured all the hardships of her husband's expedition to discover Lake Albert. Another courageous wife was Mrs Petherick, whose husband was a British consul and ivory trader on the Upper Nile. Her travels ended sadly, when her husband quarrelled with the explorer John Speke and was accused of slave-trading. The Pethericks spent their lives trying to clear their reputation. On the Upper Nile at the same time as Lady Baker was Madame Alexine Tinné, who hired a fleet of river boats—on one of which she had a grand piano. Accompanying her were her sister and daughter, several German scientists, 50 white maids, 200 African servants and the ships' crews. But malaria killed most of them.

**▼ Mrs Sheldon** was asleep in her palanquin when she woke with a sensation of "some harmful thing". A porter brought a lantern, to reveal a 15-ft. python. It was quickly killed.

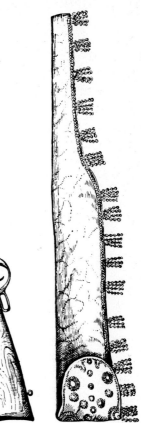

**▼ May French Sheldon's rifle** and its case, presented to her by African villagers.

**◄ May French Sheldon** met the Sultan of Zanzibar who gave her permission to travel in the interior. Their meeting is described in her book, *Sultan to Sultan.* After being offered "a quick succession of various sorts of sherbets . . . of all colours beginning with brown, closely followed by red, green, and white syrup-like fluids" (which she politely and "with suspicion" refused), the intrepid lady asked the Sultan's help in finding porters and escorts. The Sultan enlisted over 100 men to accompany her, warning them that any who deserted would have their throats cut.

As she left, he ordered his band to play "some special pieces in my honour, which, as usual, wound up the performance by the national anthem, an explosive *pot-pourri*". Then he drenched her with perfume.

## "Unladylike" explorers

Women explorers in Victorian times never thought of wearing trousers in the jungle or the desert. Mary Kingsley explained that she would rather have "mounted a public scaffold" than enter the unknown in men's garments. She sat primly in her canoe in an ankle-length, long-sleeved dress while Africans in loin-cloths paddled her through the steaming jungle lining the Ogowé River.

Even Mrs Sheldon dressed elaborately for the march into East Africa, with a cap like the one Dr Livingstone had worn, and an embroidered jacket copying the style designed by her friend Henry Stanley. Although she carried six-shooters, she was never forced to shoot anyone. Instead, she kept the Africans she met very busy posing for her camera. Many of the photographs she took were published in her book, *Sultan to Sultan.*

The women explorers were proud to be alone in command of an all-male expedition; in Victorian times a woman's job was supposed to be to stay at home and look after a family. Men explorers always took some local women along to do the cooking. Women were also a sign that an expedition was peaceful, and they were said to be good at collecting information by gossiping to the villagers. But Mrs Sheldon said that the women in her party were "a decided detriment, and caused me unceasing anxiety."

# The Rescue of Emin Pasha

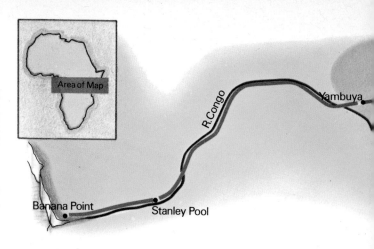

▼ **Stanley's expedition** struggles up a mountainside during the rescue of Emin Pasha. In the west-east crossing of Africa from the Congo estuary to Zanzibar, the loss of life neared 1,000. Stanley's iron will kept the expedition going. He halted desertions by public hangings.

## Stanley's expedition to rescue Emin Pasha

Emin Pasha was a mystery man. In 1885 it became known that he was governing a region called Equatoria in the Southern Sudan, with the help of 4,000 troops. Emin was cut off by followers of the Madhi, the Muslim zealot who had captured Khartoum and killed General Gordon. But Emin himself was a Muslim—of strange origins. His real name was Eduard Schnitzer, his birthplace Prussia. In Britain a campaign grew to "relieve" Emin. It was not just that he wanted help: imperialist interests hoped to make his territory part of British East Africa. Henry Stanley agreed to lead the expedition. But he was still in the pay of King Leopold of the Belgians; he also wanted Emin's "kingdom", to add to the Congo Free State.

Stanley recruited a team of army officers and plunged into Africa. He had with him 700 African porters and mercenaries, and took along the famous slave-trader Tippu Tib as an assistant. It was the biggest and most warlike expedition ever seen in Central Africa. To please Leopold, Stanley decided to reach Emin by way of the Congo, and this meant marching through the unexplored Ituri rain forest. It proved a nightmare. The expedition was attacked by pygmies with poisoned arrows, was often lost in the trackless forest, and could not find enough food.

Stanley claimed he could go through the forest and reach Emin at Lake Albert in two months; it took him six months. He then had to go back again to collect the expedition's rearguard. He lost 440 men. To cap it all, Emin did not want to be "rescued", despite a rebellion among his troops. In the end, Stanley persuaded him to be led to Zanzibar. On the way from Lake Albert to the coast, the snow-capped Ruwenzori Mountains were discovered. Stanley became a hero throughout Europe and his book *In Darkest Africa* was published in 17 countries. His feat completed the exploration of tropical Africa and speeded up colonialism. Most of Equatoria became part of what is now Uganda. Emin joined the German colonial service, went back to the Ituri region and there was murdered by a slave trader.

◀ **The 6,000-mile journey** included a long steamer trip up the Congo River. Stanley had to leave part of his force behind at Yambuya while he hurried on to help Emin. When he went back to find them, only 60 out of 270 men were still alive.

▼ **After this last expedition** in his 20 years of African travel, Stanley stopped in Cairo to write a book about it. But hundreds of telegrams flooded in congratulating him and asking if he would make speeches when he reached Britain. Stanley's servant, Sali Ben Othman, would nervously poke them into the room on the end of a bamboo pole, then runaway followed by shouts of "I detest telegrams!" Stanley settled in London, became an M.P. and was knighted. He died in 1904.

▲ **When Stanley and Emin met** beside Lake Albert, the rescuer was much worse off than the man he had come so far to help. Emin had managed, although cut off for years, to run his province efficiently. With his thick spectacles, Emin seemed to Stanley like a professor of law. They soon quarrelled.

▶ **The happiest moment** for Stanley and his men was when they at last hacked through the Ituri forest and emerged in open country. But soon they were fighting with suspicious tribesmen whose lands they were entering. Although no white-led expeditions had penetrated the region, Arab slave-raiders made the inhabitants hostile. Stanley executed one of his men for selling a rifle.

# The Africans' View of the Explorers

The Europeans said they were "discovering" Africa. But the Africans knew its "secrets" all the time. They found the explorers puzzling—and sometimes frightening.

**The Hunters.** Africa was full of big game. Wealthy white men shot animals for pleasure. Others were after ivory.

**The Arabs.** They came to trade and to buy slaves. Others came to spread the Koran.

**The Settlers.** Most Europeans travelled through Africa and went away again. But in South Africa the white settlers came to stay.

**The Missionaries.** They devoted themselves to winning converts to Christianity. Africans were told to give up their old way of life.

◄ **The white man's clothes** came to show authority. That is why King Moshesh of Basutoland, over 100 years ago, wore a top hat. The King of Barotseland wore an admiral's uniform.

38

## An African viewpoint

White travellers in Africa often did not realize that they looked as strange to the Africans as the Africans did to them. The explorers were always given nicknames by the porters working for them, usually those of animals or birds they most resembled. The explorers generally believed that all Africans looked up to them as a "superior race". It is true that modern European weapons caused amazement. Also, the Africans were eager to learn the white skills of reading and writing—that is why the missionaries were welcomed. But the chiefs were men of dignity. They demanded tribute (called, *hongo* in East Africa) from any white man who wanted to march through their territory. The King of Bonny, at the mouth of the Niger River, wrote complaining to King George IV of a warship patrolling near his capital. He addressed the British ruler on equal terms: "Brudder Georges". Only a few Africans could, until modern times, put their thoughts about the foreign travellers and traders in writing. One who did learn to do so was a freed slave called Ignatius Sancho. In 1783 he gave his views on slavery. "But the poor Africans, to whom the Lord has granted a rich and 'Luxuriant' land, are the most unhappy section of humanity on account of the slave trade; and it is the Christians who are responsible."

**The Soldiers.** When the European nations began to rule Africa, they sent army expeditions to explore and control the wilder parts of Africa.

▼ **A humorous view** of Europeans is shown in these carvings from West Africa. From left to right: a cavalry officer, a missionary's wife and child, a district officer, and

Queen Victoria. The Great White Queen had several places named after her—such as Lake Victoria and the Victoria Falls.

# Naturalist's Notebook

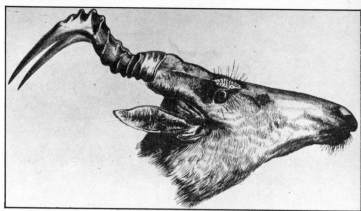

◀ One of the finest recorders of African wildlife was **William Cornwallis Harris,** an army officer who in 1836 went to the Cape from India to restore his health. He travelled 1,000 miles inland, going far beyond the outposts of the *Voortrekkers* (the Boer farmers who set off from the Cape to settle new lands). He portrayed their way of life (left) between painting and shooting animals.
He was a vivid artist and his paintings were published in 1840.

▲ **Drawing of an antelope** by Georg Schweinfurth, a Prussian explorer, who spent three years in Central Africa, 1868-71, and brought back an unrivalled array of plant life and insects. He also studied wild animals, and his two-volume book about his travels ends with a list of more than 70 that he identified, with their Latin and African names. When his crates of plants and insects were lost in a fire near the end of his journey, he doggedly made a fresh collection.

▼ **Zebra on the African plains.** This painting by Baines captures the beauty of the game that once roamed freely all across the continent. Naturalists of the last century did not foresee the massive slaughter of wildlife which modern rifles would bring about. Many species are threatened with extinction.

▲ **Antelope** painted in 1849 at St Lucia Bay, Natal, by George Franck Angas. Africa has more than 60 species of hoofed animals. There are 9 types of giraffe, the world's tallest animal, and 45 varieties of African monkeys. The world's fastest animal is the African cheetah. which can reach 60 m.p.h., and the biggest primate is the gorilla of the Eastern Congo.

▼ **Thomas Baines,** an adventurer from Norfolk was a self-taught artist. He made some paintings of the Victoria Falls (one is shown below) after being dismissed from Livingstone's expedition. Baines was also a crack shot. A companion was with him while he was sketching plants along the Zambezi: "Suddenly he dropped his pencil and sketch book, seized his gun, and shot a tiger cat that had intruded; upon which he resumed his pencil as if nothing had occurred".

## Naturalists in Africa

After more than two centuries, the continent's twelve million square miles still offer surprises to the botanist and zoologist. For example, Africa has 1,700 known types of birds, but new ones are still being discovered. First in the field during the era of exploration were the botanists. In 1772, an expedition northwards from the Cape was organized by Carl Per Thunberg, a Swedish botanist, and Francis Masson, a Scot. On their trip they found 400 unknown species of plants. By the middle of the last century, zoos were thriving all over Europe and the United States and receiving specimens from Africa.

Some of the best reports of the teeming animal and plant life in the interior came from the explorers themselves. David Livingstone and Samuel Baker were both keen observers. So were many big game hunters, such as William Baldwin, who became the second white man to see the Victoria Falls—finding his way with a pocket compass and narrowly escaping death from the jaws of a crocodile. The German travellers were more scholarly in their studies of the flora and fauna: outstanding among them was Dr Heinrich Barth. Today they would, sadly enough, find less to record.

# The Archaeologist Explorers

One hundred years ago in Africa, explorers were looking for the Source of the Nile. Today they are looking for the Source of Mankind. Fragments of bone are being put together to make the skulls of early man like the one below, found in Kenya.

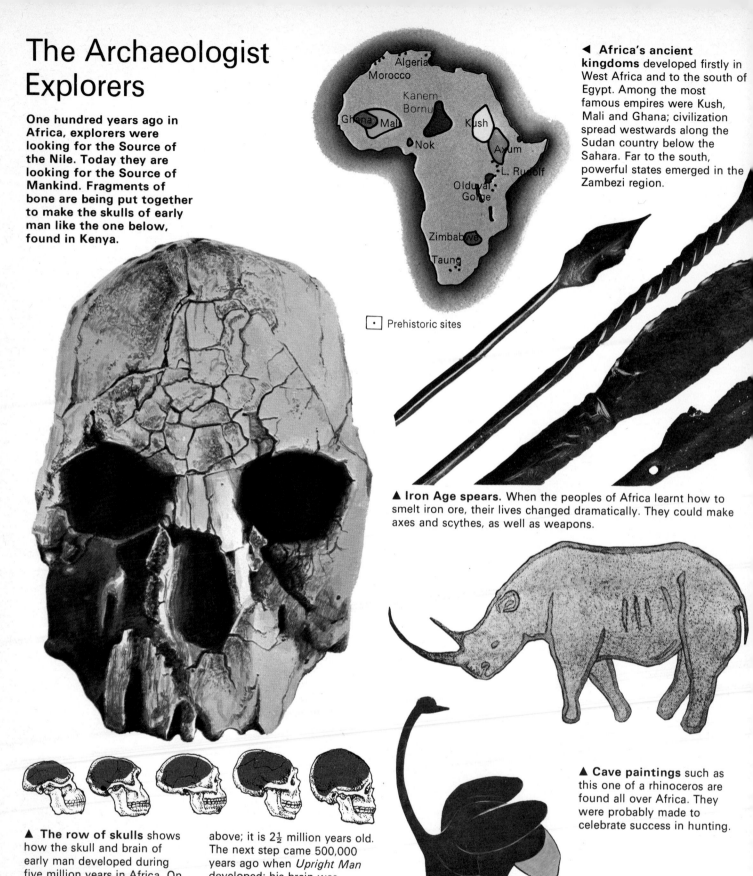

◄ **Africa's ancient kingdoms** developed firstly in West Africa and to the south of Egypt. Among the most famous empires were Kush, Mali and Ghana; civilization spread westwards along the Sudan country below the Sahara. Far to the south, powerful states emerged in the Zambezi region.

· Prehistoric sites

▲ **Iron Age spears.** When the peoples of Africa learnt how to smelt iron ore, their lives changed dramatically. They could make axes and scythes, as well as weapons.

▲ **Cave paintings** such as this one of a rhinoceros are found all over Africa. They were probably made to celebrate success in hunting.

◄ **Once ostriches** were found in the Sahara. Now they are mostly found in South Africa, where this rock painting was discovered.

▲ **The row of skulls** shows how the skull and brain of early man developed during five million years in Africa. On left is the ape man called *Australopithecus*. His brain was less than 500 cubic centimetres—not much bigger than a chimpanzee's. Next came "1470 Man", with a brain of 800 c.c. This skull is another view of the large one above; it is 2½ million years old. The next step came 500,000 years ago when *Upright Man* developed; his brain was two-thirds of the size of modern man's. The fourth skull is of *Neanderthal Man,* who lived 70,000 years ago. Finally, 30,000 years ago, modern man *(Homo Sapiens Sapiens)* arrived with his 1,450 c.c. brain.

## Digging up Africa's past

The early explorers discovered much about the geography and life of Africa, but they never guessed that Africa was the place where mankind began. The leading "archaeologist explorer" in Africa, Dr Louis Leakey, discovered in the Olduvai Gorge in Tanzania the pieces of bone that have been fitted together to form the skulls of our most distant ancestors—the earliest men. There is strong evidence that mankind first lived around the area of Lake Victoria. Undoubtedly, many more discoveries about Africa's first men will be made in future years.

Archaeology teaches us much about the life and history of ancient peoples. We know that as the ages passed, the climate of the world changed. The Sahara was once fit for human habitation, for the people who lived there left behind them many wall paintings of warriors and animals.

We also know that a few thousand years ago, groups of people spread out from the Nile Valley, taking with them their knowledge of growing crops and working with metals. Soon the skill of making iron, for use in spears and farming tools, spread all over the continent, even to the extreme south. Archaeology also tells us that sailors came across the Indian Ocean many centuries ago to settle in Madagascar and parts of East Africa. These sailors were really some of the first explorers, and they are thought to have come from Sumatra. Bones, pots and weapons dug up in West Africa are revealing much to us about the empires that flourished there. So the exploration of Africa goes on. Instead of venturing into its "blank spaces" men are now making discoveries in time, looking far into Africa's mysterious past.

▶ **An exciting discovery** by archaeologists in Nigeria: heads and statues of the Nok culture, more than 2,000 years old, and made of terracotta (baked earth).

▼ **The Zimbabwe ruins** in the south of what is now Rhodesia. They date from about A.D. 200, and nobody knows exactly who built them. The stonework is adorned with a zig-zag pattern and the centre of the ruins is a massive citadel.

**They believed in "white supremacy"**

▼ **Bismark** established German colonies in Africa. They were lost in World War One.

▼ **Cecil Rhodes** occupied the country now named after him. He made a fortune from gold.

▼ **Kruger** believed in independence for the Boers in South Africa.

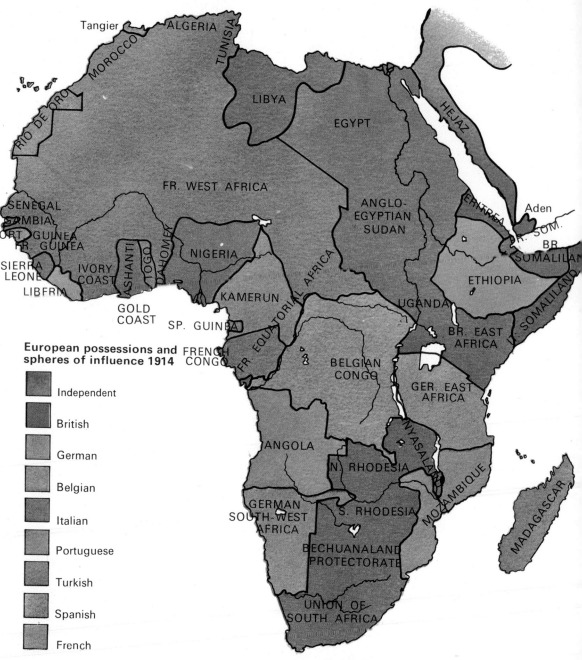

**European possessions and spheres of influence 1914**

- Independent
- British
- German
- Belgian
- Italian
- Portuguese
- Turkish
- Spanish
- French

Map labels: Tangier, MOROCCO, RIO DE ORO, ALGERIA, TUNISIA, LIBYA, EGYPT, HEJAZ, ERITREA, Aden, SENEGAL, GAMBIA, PORT GUINEA, FR. GUINEA, SIERRA LEONE, LIBERIA, IVORY COAST, ASHANTI, GOLD COAST, TOGO, DAHOMEY, NIGERIA, SP. GUINEA, KAMERUN, FR. WEST AFRICA, ANGLO-EGYPTIAN SUDAN, ETHIOPIA, BR. SOM., BR. SOMALILAND, UGANDA, IT. SOMALILAND, BR. EAST AFRICA, FRENCH CONGO, FR. EQUATORIAL AFRICA, BELGIAN CONGO, GER. EAST AFRICA, ANGOLA, NYASALAND, N. RHODESIA, MOZAMBIQUE, GERMAN SOUTH-WEST AFRICA, S. RHODESIA, BECHUANALAND PROTECTORATE, MADAGASCAR, UNION OF SOUTH AFRICA

▼ **Sierra Leone, 1909:** family life, colonial style. White rule gave way to independent Africa in less than a century.

## The scramble for Africa

Many Africans view the white explorers and their achievements with mixed feelings. After the explorations came the occupations. By 1900 the whole of Africa was under white rule except for Liberia and Ethiopia. All the shapes drawn on the map of Africa came from white bargaining, in which the peoples of Africa took no part. The bargaining began at the Conference of Berlin in 1884; it was called by Bismark, the German Chancellor, to "carve up" Africa into regions where one or another of the European powers could rule.

In some cases the explorers helped to lead the new administrators. Henry Stanley ran the Congo Free

# Africa 1970

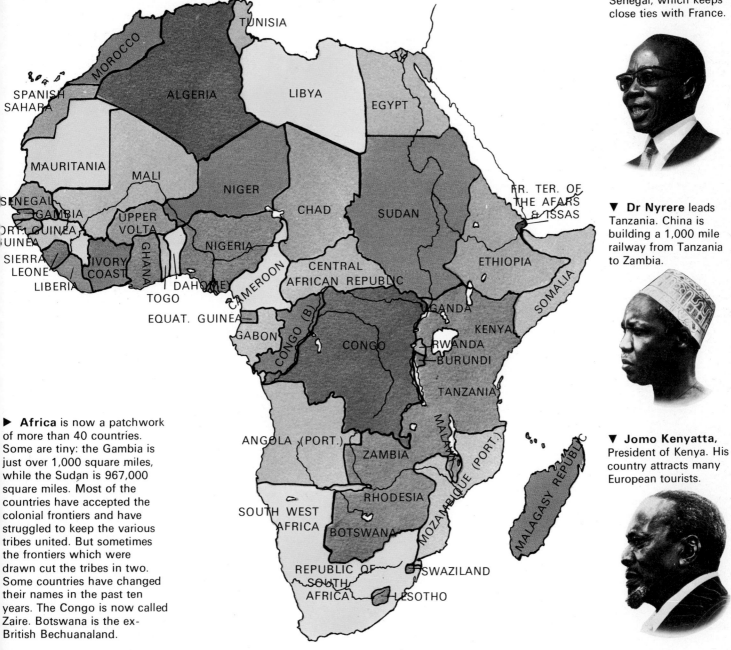

▼ **Leopold Senghor,** poet and President of Senegal, which keeps close ties with France.

▼ **Dr Nyrere** leads Tanzania. China is building a 1,000 mile railway from Tanzania to Zambia.

▼ **Jomo Kenyatta,** President of Kenya. His country attracts many European tourists.

► **Africa** is now a patchwork of more than 40 countries. Some are tiny: the Gambia is just over 1,000 square miles, while the Sudan is 967,000 square miles. Most of the countries have accepted the colonial frontiers and have struggled to keep the various tribes united. But sometimes the frontiers which were drawn cut the tribes in two. Some countries have changed their names in the past ten years. The Congo is now called Zaire. Botswana is the ex-British Bechuanaland.

State. A German traveller, Carl Peters, made treaties with the chiefs of East Africa for Germany. In West Africa, British traders helped to create Nigeria for Britain. Count de Brazza planted the French flag on the north bank of the Congo.

## The road to independence

World War One, 1914–18, changed the map of Africa. Germany was the loser and had to give up her colonies by the terms of peace. World War Two brought more changes; many Africans were called up to fight and they were given the chance to see many parts of the world. They came back home with new ideas. At the end of the war, Italy lost its colonies. But soon all the European countries were to start

leaving the territories they had "discovered" at the end of the 19th century. By 1960, most of Africa was independent.

One place which is greatly changed is Zanzibar, the island where many explorers began their journeys. The *dhows* still sail between Zanzibar and the mainland, but they no longer carry elephant tusks and slaves. Instead they transport manufactured goods from all over the world. The Sultan of Zanzibar, the descendant of the ruler who allowed Burton and Speke to venture into the interior, has been deposed. He now lives in a seaside town in England.

# Time Chart: Africa's Explorers

This time chart shows that the bulk of the organized exploration of Africa took place in the 19th century.

▶ **Speke and Grant** reached Buganda, to the west of Lake Victoria, in 1862. In the picture, Grant is dancing with the Queen Mother of Buganda.

| | |
|---|---|
| **400 B.C.** | A fleet of 60 Phoenician ships, commanded by Hanno, sail down the West African coast, perhaps as far as the Equator. |
| **A.D 600** | Arabs begin conquest of North Africa and build towns along the East Coast as far as Zanzibar and Mozambique. |
| **1054** | Arab armies cross the Sahara into West Africa and conquer the ancient state of Ghana. Timbuktu founded. |
| **1350** | Ibn Battuta, an Arab traveller, visits East and West Africa and writes an account of his explorations. |
| **1415** | Prince Henry of Portugal (the "Navigator") captures Ceuta in North Africa from the Arabs and orders his sailors to go south. |
| **1498** | Vasco da Gama sails around the Cape and reaches India. The Portuguese control the African coastline. |

| | |
|---|---|
| **1768** | James Bruce begins his travels to Ethiopia where he visits the source of the Blue Nile. |
| **1795** | Mungo Park goes to West Africa and reaches the Niger River. He dies on his second exploration, 1,000 miles down-river. |
| **1798** | Francesco de Lacerda travels up the Zambezi and reaches the capital of King Kazembe, where he dies. |
| **1822** | Hugh Clapperton crosses the Sahara to Sokoto. He dies there on his second exploration to the Niger. |
| **1827** | Disguised as an Arab, René Caillié reaches Timbuktu and makes a south-north crossing of the Sahara. |
| **1830** | Richard and John Lander trace the course of the Niger River to the Atlantic. |
| **1848** | The missionary Johan Rebmann travels inland from Mombasa and sees the snow-covered peak of Kilimanjaro. |

| | |
|---|---|
| **1849** | David Livingstone begins exploring. With two hunters, Murray and Oswell, he discovers Lake Ngami. |
| **1851** | Livingstone and his family journey north to the Zambezi River and are welcomed by Chief Sebituane. |
| **1855** | First crossing of Africa by a white explorer: on the way, Livingstone sees the Victoria Falls. |
| **1858** | Richard Burton and John Speke reach Lake Tanganyika. Search for the Nile has begun. |
| **1862** | Speke and James Grant reach Buganda beside Lake Victoria. Speke discovers the Ripon Falls. |
| **1864** | Sir Samuel and Lady Baker arrive at Lake Albert after travelling up the Nile. |
| **1864** | Livingstone completes his Zambezi expedition, during which he explored Lake Malawi. |

| | |
|---|---|
| **1871** | Henry Stanley sets out from Zanzibar and discovers Livingstone at Ujiji. They sail on Lake Tanganyika. |
| **1873** | Livingstone dies at Chitambo on his way to Lake Bangweulu, and his body is carried to the coast by his African followers. |
| **1877** | Stanley sails down the Congo River to the Atlantic and so completes crossing of Central Africa from east to west. |
| **1880** | Christian missionaries begin establishing stations in the heart of the continent. |
| **1882** | Joseph Thompson, a Scottish geologist, penetrates Masai country to find a direct route to Lake Victoria, from the East Coast. |
| **1888** | Last great expedition; Stanley crosses Africa for the second time to rescue Emin Pasha, the Governor of Equatoria, from the Sudan. |

# Index

Entries in **bold** refer to illustrations.

Albert, Lake, 22, **23**, 25, **25**, 32, 36-7
Almoravids, 21
Angola, 8, **9**, 12
animals, for transport, 6, **6-7**, 25, 27; skins for trade, 16; *see also* wildlife
Arabs, 4-5, 13, 16, 19, 22, 29, **38**, *see also* Islam
archaeology, 42-3, **42-3**
art, African, 10-11, **10-11**, 42

Baines, Thomas, 18, **18**, **40-1**
Baker, Samuel and Florence, 22, 24-5, **24-5**, 32, 34, 41
Baldwin, William, 41
Bangweulu, Lake, 28, **29**
Bantu, **11**
Baptista, 8-9
Baker, Frederick, 32, **33**
barter, 17, **16-17**
Barth, Heinrich, **30**, 41
beads, for trading, 16-17, **17**
Benin, **10**
Berlin, Conference of, 44
Bismark, German Chancellor, 44, **44**
Blood River, battle of, 14
Blue Nile, River, **7**, 8-9, **23**
Boers, 14-15, **14-15**, 18, **18**, 44
Bonny, King of, 39
Brazil, **12**, 13
Britain, 9, 15
Bruce, James, 8-9, **8**, 23
Burton, Richard, 22, **22-3**
Bushmen, **11**, 15

Cabora Bassa Rapids, 19, **19**
Caillié, René, **6**
Cam, Diego, 4
camels, 6, **7**, 16, 27
cameras, used by explorers, 27, 30, 35
Cape of Good Hope, Cape Colony, 4, **5**, 14-15, **14-15**
Cape Town, 15
caravan routes, 6, **6**
carvings, African, **10**, **39**
cave art, **42**
Chad, Lake, 6
China, 16, 45
Chitambo, village of, **29**
Christians, 4-5, 20-1, **20-1**, 23, *see also* missionaries
Chuma, **28**
cloth, used in trade, 6, 12, 16-17, **16-17**
clothes, explorers', 26-7, **26-7**, **38**
colonization, 44-5, **44-5**; of Americas, 6, 13; of Congo, 32-3; of East Africa, 36, 45; of South Africa, 14-15; of West Africa, 45
compass, **4**, 30, **31**, 41
Congo, Belgian, 32, 36, 44, **44**

Congo River, 4-6, **7**, 23, 27, 32, **32**
copper, 16
Cornwallis-Harris, **30**, 40
Crowther, Bishop, **13**
Cushite language, 11

da Gama, Vasco, 4-5, **4**, 15
Darwin, Charles, 30
de Brazza, Count Savorgnan, 32, **33**, 45
De Lacerda, Francisco, 8-9
Diaz, Bartholomew, 4-5
Dinka, **23**
diseases, 6, 14, 19, 21, **33**, 34
Drakensberg Mountains, **7**, 14-15
du Chaillu, Paul, 30
Dutch colonists, 14-15, **14-15**, 16

ebony, 16
Egypt, 11, 22, 25
Emin Pasha, (Eduard Schnitzer), 36-7, **37**
Equatoria, 36
Ethiopia, **7**, 8-9, 16, **21**, **23**, 44

France, 6, 15, 30, 32

Galton, Francis, 27, 30
Gambia River, 9
Germany, 22, 30, 44
Ghana, 11, 21, **42**
gold, 4, 16
Gondokoro, 25, **25**
Gordon, General Charles, 21, 25
Grant, James, 22, **22-3**, 25, 32
Great Trek, 15, **14-15**
Great Triangle, 12-13, **12**
guns, *see* weapons

Hamites, **11**
Henry, Prince of Portugal, the Navigator, 4-5, **4**
Hottentots, **11**, **14**, 15
hunters, **38**

India, 4-5, 16
instruments, scientific, **9**, 30-1, **31**
Iron Age, 11, **42**
Islam, 4, 6, 21, **21**, 36, *see also* Arabs
Italy, 45
Ituri rain forest, 36
ivory, 16-17, **16-17**, 34, 38

Johnston, James, 27
José, 8-9

Kalahari Desert, **7**, 15, 18
Kamrasi, 25
Kazembe, Lunda king, **9**
Kenya, 42, 45
Kenya, Mount, **7**
Kenyatta, Jomo, **45**
Khartoum, 21, 23, **23**, 25
Khedive Ismail, **23**, 25
Kilimanjaro, Mount, **7**, 34
Kingsley, Mary, **34**, 35
Kitchener, General, 21
Kolobeng, 18, **18-19**
Koran, the, 21, 38

Krapf, 22
Kruger, Paul, **44**
Kush, 42

Lalibela, king, 23
Leakey, Dr Louis, 43
Leopold II of Belgium, 32, **33**, 36
Livingstone, David, 18-19, **18-19**, 21-2, 28-9, **28-9**, 30-1, 41
Lualaba, River, 29, 32

Madhi, the, 21, 25, 36
Mali, 11, **42**
Manza, king, **31**
Maria Theresa dollar, **16**
*Ma Robert*, the, 19, **19**
Masson, Francis, 41
medicine, **26**, **28**
missionaries, 9, **13**, 18-19, 20-1, **20-1**, 26, **38**, 39, **39**
Mombasa, 5, **5**, 22
Morocco, 4, **5**
Mosesh, king, **38**
"Mountains of the Moon", 22, *see also* Ruwenzori
Mozambique, 8, **9**
Murchison Falls, 24-5, **24**
music, African, 11, **10-11**
Muslims, *see* Islam
Mutesa, king of Buganda, 17, **23**

naturalists, 40-1, **40-1**
Negroes, **10**
Niger, River, 6, **7-8**, 8-9, 39
Nigeria, 10, 21, 43, 45
Nile River, 6-7, **7**, 9; search for the source of, 22-3, **22-3**, 24-5, 28-9
Nok, **42-3**
Nyasa, Lake, 19, **19**, 22
Nyerere, Dr, **45**

Ogowé River, 34-5
Orange River, 15, **15**
Othman dan Fodio, 21

Park, Mungo, 8-9, **8**
Peters, Carl, 45
Petherick, Katherine, 34, **34**
Phoenicians, 4
plants, 30, **30**, 40-1
Pocock, Frank and Edward, 32, **33**
Portugal, 4-5, **4-5**, 9, 16, 19
Prester John, **21**
Ptolemy, 22
pygmies, **20**, 30, 36

Rebmann, 22
Red Sea, **8**, 9, 16
religions, African, 11, 21, *see also* Islam, Christianity
Rhodes, Cecil, **44**
Ripon Falls, 22, **23**, 25
Romans, 11
Royal Geographical Society, 22, 25, 29
Ruwenzori Mountains, **7**, **23**, 36, **37**

Sahara Desert, 6, **7**, 13, 42-3
Schweinfurth, Georg, **30**, 31, 40

scientists, 30-1, **30-1**
Senghor, Leopold, **45**
sextant, 30, **31**
Sheldon, May French, 35, **34-5**
ships, 4-5, **4-5**, 12-13, **12-13**
slave trade, the, 12-13, **12-13**, 15, 16-17, **19**, 29, 34, 38
Somaliland, 22
South Africa, 10, 14-15, **14-15**
Spain, 4-6
Speke, John, 22, **22-3**, 25, 32, 34
Stanley, Henry, 27, 29, **29**, 32-3, **32-3**, 36-7, **37**, 44
Sudan, 21, 23, 25, 36
Sudd, the, **23**
Susi, 28

Tana, Lake, **7-8**, 8, **23**
Tanganyika, Lake, **7**, 22-3, **23**, 29, 32
telescope, **9**
Tete, 9, **9**
thermometer, boiling a, **31**
Thomson, Joseph, 31
Thunberg, Carl Per, 41
Timbuktu, 6, **7**, 21
Tinné, Alexine & Alexandrine, 34, **34**
Tippu Tib, **33**, 36
trade and traders, 4, 6, 11, 16-17, **16-17**
transport, **6-7**, 27
Transvaal, 14, **15**
tribes, African, 11, **10-11**
Tuaregs, **6**, 34
Turkey, 25

Uganda, 25, 36
Ujiji, 22, 29, **29**
United States, **12**, 13

van der Stel, Simon, 15
van Riebeeck, Jan & Maria, **14**, 15
Victoria Falls, 18-19, **18-19**, 39, 41
Victoria, Lake, 22-3, **23**, 24-5, 32. 43
*Voortrekkers*, 14-15, **14-15**, 40

weapons, Portuguese, 5, **5**; used in trade, 6, 12, 17; used by explorers, **9**, **26**, **33**, 35, **35**, 39; used by colonists, 14, 15
West Indies, **12**, 13
Wilberforce, William, 13
wildlife, African, 23, 26, 30, **30**, **35**, 38, 40-1, **40-1**

Zambezi, River, 6, **7**, 9, 18-19, **18-19**
Zanzibar, **16**, 17, 29, **29**, 32-3, 36-7, 45
Zanzibar, Sultan of, **34-5**, 45
Zimbabwe, 11, **43**
Zulus, **14**, 15